Outside front cover:
(top left, and page 10) Cullen Skink; *(top right, and pages 36 and 35)* Tillypronie Honey Cakes and Treacle Scones; *(bottom left, and page 31)* Crannachan; *(bottom right, and page 23)* Venison Casserole; *(background picture and opposite)* Eilean Donan Castle, near Dornie, Highland.

Outside back cover:
(top) Tobermory, Isle of Mull; *(centre, and page 17)* Salmon Kedgeree; *(bottom, and page 40)* Dundee Cake.

In the same series:
A Taste of Norfolk by Mary Norwak

Photography by John Brooks
© Jarrold Publishing 1999

ISBN 0-7117-1099-6
© Jarrold Publishing 1999
Designed and produced
by Jarrold Publishing, Norwich.
Printed in Spain. 1/99

A · LITTLE BOOK · OF

Scottish

RECIPES

by Mary Norwak

JARROLD
PUBLISHING

*Crannachan (page 31)
and Shortbread (page 37)*

CONTENTS

Introduction

THE NORTHERN climate of Scotland is not hospitable, and about one-third of the land is unsuitable for agriculture, but the country is famous for the high quality of its produce, and there is plenty of good food to be found. The climate is against the growing of cereals, except for oats which have always thrived in poor conditions. Oats are used for the famous breakfast porridge, but are also used for breads and biscuits, for thickening meat mixtures such as haggis and sausages, for puddings and even for drinks. Fish abounds, and the Scots have developed the art of preparing and smoking fish for short-term storage – they used to provide travelling girls who dealt with the English herring harvest as well as their own. There is fine beef and lamb, and the smokehouse skills are used to provide fine bacon from local pigs. Potatoes and root vegetables grow well, and Scottish raspberries are famous.

Fine whisky is exported all over the world, but it often slips into special dishes in restaurants and home kitchens. Historically, the basic Scottish diet was plain and perhaps a little dull, but the country forged the Auld Alliance with France, which influenced the kitchen to produce for the professional and upper classes some very fine dishes that are still much in favour.

Tobermory, Mull

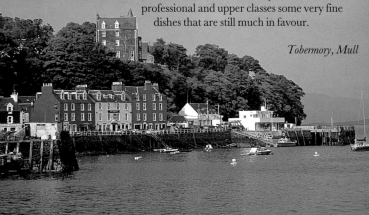

Soups

The Scots have created a number of famous soups that are much enjoyed in their cold climate. They are clever in using chicken, fish and root vegetables to make filling, chunky soups that are almost complete meals, but which have distinctive character and style. It is possible that their ideas derive from French recipes, for the French are just as fond of their huge tureens of tasty and nourishing soup.

PARTAN BREE
SERVES 4–6

8 oz (225g) brown and white crabmeat
1 pint (600ml) milk
3 oz (75g) rice
1 pint (600ml) water
salt and freshly ground white pepper
few drops of anchovy essence
1/4 pint (150ml) single cream

Separate the brown and white crabmeat, and keep half the white meat on one side. Put the milk into a pan and bring to the boil. Add the rice, bring to the boil, cover and then simmer until the rice is soft. Stir in the crabmeat and then liquidise until creamy, or put through a sieve. Return to the pan with the water and bring to the boil. Season well with salt, pepper and anchovy essence, and stir in the reserved white crabmeat. Heat gently but do not boil. Stir in the cream and serve at once.

'Partan' is a crab and 'bree' means liquid, and this distinctive soup is a good way of making the best of crabmeat. For a really fine flavour a freshly boiled crab should be used, but if not available frozen crabmeat may be used.

This is a filling soup from Cullen, near Seatown. For the best flavour it should be made from a whole finnan haddock with bones and skin, but otherwise a fillet of smoked haddock can be used. 'Skink' is an old word for soup or broth.

CULLEN SKINK

SERVES 4

1 large finnan haddock
(or 8 oz (225g) smoked fillet)
1 medium onion
salt and pepper
2 pints (1 litre) water
1/2 pint (300ml) milk
2 oz (50g) butter
1 lb (450g) potatoes
4 tablespoons single cream
chopped fresh parsley

Put the fish into a large pan. Peel and chop the onion, and add to the pan with salt, pepper and water. Bring to the boil, cover and simmer for 20 minutes. Peel and boil the potatoes and mash them well.

Drain the fish, keeping the cooking-liquid. Remove the skin and bone from the fish. Strain the cooking-liquid and return to the pan with the mashed potatoes. Add the milk and butter and the flaked fish. Bring to the boil, cover and simmer for 5 minutes. Garnish with a spoonful of cream in each dish and a little parsley.

Cullen Skink

This soup has been made in Scotland for hundreds of years, and is a mixture of beef and chicken, well-flavoured with leeks, and with the addition of prunes. The prunes are not always used these days but they do add a delicious and unusual flavour. For a cheaper version of the soup, beef stock may be used without the meat, but originally a slice each of beef and chicken were served in the broth.

COCK-A-LEEKIE
SERVES 8–10

2 lb (1kg) shin beef
    or 4 pints (2 litres) beef stock
1 large chicken
2 lb (1kg) leeks
18 prunes
salt and pepper

If using beef, put it into a large pan with 4 pints (2 litres) water, cover and simmer for 2 hours before adding the chicken. If not, put the chicken into hot stock to start the soup. Clean the leeks and put in half of them tied into a bundle. Bring to the boil, cover and simmer for 1 hour. Add the prunes and continue simmering for 30 minutes and then remove the chicken (and beef if used). Slice the remaining leeks and add to the pan. Boil for 2 minutes. Season well. Discard the bundle of leeks. Serve a slice each of beef and chicken in soup plates and cover with broth, sliced leeks and prunes. For convenient serving it is easiest to cut the sliced beef and chicken into small pieces.

There will be plenty of meat left over for other meals.

Scotch Broth
SERVES 8

3 lb (1.5kg) lamb neck, ribs and knuckle
4 oz (100g) pearl barley
4 oz (100g) split peas
2 medium carrots
2 medium onions
2 young turnips or 1 small swede
2½ pints (1.5 litres) water
salt and pepper
chopped fresh parsley

A wonderfully filling soup that is a complete meal and very nourishing with its mixture of meat, vegetables, pulses and cereal.

Put the meat into a large pan with the water and add barley and peas. Bring slowly to the boil and skim until clear, then cover and simmer for 30 minutes. Add diced carrots, onions and turnips or swede, and continue simmering for about 1 hour until the meat is tender.

Remove the meat and strip off the flesh. Chop finely and return to the pan. Reheat, adding plenty of salt and pepper, and serve garnished with parsley.

FISH

Fishing has always been an important Scottish industry, and the haddock and herring are much prized. Kippers and smoked haddock have greatly enhanced the reputation of Scottish food. Crabs are the favourite shellfish, and are made into some unusual dishes such as soup. The king of fish is undoubtedly the salmon.

In the 19th century, when wild salmon was plentiful, this was a common dish sold in cookshops and known as 'Salmon Hash'. It was so good, however, that it was also enjoyed in inns and country-houses under the grander name of Tweed Kettle, since most of the fish came from the River Tweed.

TWEED KETTLE

SERVES 6

3 lb (1.5kg) salmon
2 shallots
1/2 pint (300ml) dry white wine
pinch of ground mace
2 tablespoons fresh parsley
salt and freshly ground pepper

Put the salmon into a deep pan and just cover with water. Bring slowly to the boil and simmer for 1 minute. Lift the salmon out of the pan, reserving the cooking-liquid. Remove the skin and bones and discard. Cut the salmon into 2 in (5cm) cubes.

Measure the cooking-liquid and put 1/2 pint (300ml) into a clean pan. Add the salmon pieces. Chop the shallots finely and add along with the wine and mace. Cover and simmer for 25 minutes. Season well and stir in the parsley. Serve hot with mashed potatoes, or cold with mayonnaise.

HAM AND HADDIE

SERVES 2

2 finnan haddock
8 oz (225g) bacon rashers
1 oz (25g) butter
salt and pepper
2 tablespoons cream

Fish is very good when cooked traditionally with bacon, which is often known as 'ham' in Scotland.

Line a grill pan with foil and grease well with butter. Place the fish in the pan and dot with the remaining butter. Season lightly with salt and pepper.

Put the grid in the pan and top with bacon rashers. Grill until the bacon is cooked through, then remove and keep warm. Continue grilling for 5 minutes. Put the haddock on to serving-plates and top with bacon. Pour the pan juices and cream over it.

Smoked haddock is a glory of the Scottish kitchen. The 'finnie' originated around Aberdeen, near Findon. This is a medium-sized fish split open, brined and cold-smoked to give a delicate flavour, best appreciated when cooked in milk and dressed with butter.

The Arbroath 'smokie' is beheaded but not split. It is then dry-salted and the fish tied in pairs by their tails before hanging over hot smoke for 45 minutes, resulting in a mildly smoked copper-coloured fish. Smokies may be eaten cold with brown bread and butter, or gently heated in the oven to serve with boiled potatoes.

15

Salmon Kedgeree

SALMON KEDGEREE

SERVES 4

4 oz (100g) long-grain rice
8 oz (225g) cooked salmon
2 oz (50g) butter
2 hard-boiled eggs
3 tablespoons single cream
salt and freshly ground white pepper
pinch of Cayenne pepper
2 teaspoons chopped fresh parsley

Cook the rice in a pan of boiling salted
water until just tender. Drain very well
and keep warm. Flake the salmon. Melt
the butter and stir in the salmon. Chop the
eggs finely and stir into the pan. Remove
from the heat and stir in the cream and
plenty of salt, pepper and Cayenne
pepper. Stir into the rice and pile in a
pyramid on a hot serving-dish. Sprinkle
with parsley and serve at once.

The mixture of rice
and fish, eggs, butter
and seasoning is
supposed to derive
from recipes brought
back by those who
had served in India in
the 18th century. It
used to be a popular
breakfast dish after
parties and balls, but
today it makes a
splendid luncheon
or supper.

Meat, Game and Poultry

Scotland is famous for its game, beef and lamb. In the lowlands, there are the great Aberdeen Angus cattle that produce some of the finest beef at the age of one to two years, while the Highland cattle are not eaten until they are four years old. On the Borders, the lambs have produced meat while the wool has been the basis of another great industry of spinning, weaving and knitting. The lamb has been traditionally eaten in its mature state as mutton.

These pasties have a rich crust and a tasty filling of good Aberdeen Angus beef. It is said that the name comes from Maggie Bridie, who used to sell them at fairs and markets, but it may come from the oval shape, which resembles a 'birdie'.

Forfar Bridies
Serves 4

12 oz (350g) plain flour
3 oz (75g) margarine
3 oz (75g) lard
1 lb (450g) rump steak or topside beef
3 oz (75g) shredded suet
2 medium onions
salt and pepper

Preheat oven to 200°C/400°F/Gas Mark 6. Rub margarine and lard into the flour. Add a little salt and enough cold water to make a firm dough. Divide into 4 equal pieces and roll out into ovals.

Beat out the steak to make it thinner and cut into small squares. Mix the meat and suet and add the finely chopped onion. Season well and divide into 4 portions. Cover half of each oval with meat and seal well. Crimp the edges with fingers and thumb. Make a small hole in the top of each one. Place on a greased baking-sheet and bake for 45 minutes.

*Forfar Bridies and
Little Mutton Pies (page 20)*

These pies were old-fashioned 'fast food', popular when sold on the streets to Glasgow workers. Sometimes the rim around the lid of each hot baked pie was filled with gravy, mashed potato and peas or beans to make a complete meal. Richly flavoured mutton is not often found now, but lean lamb may be used instead.

LITTLE MUTTON PIES

12 oz (350g) plain flour
1 teaspoon salt
5 oz (125g) lard
¹/₄ pint (150ml) mixed milk and water
1 lb (450g) lean mutton or lamb
1 medium onion
1 teaspoon mushroom ketchup
2 teaspoons chopped fresh parsley
salt and freshly ground black pepper
water or stock
1 tablespoon plain flour

Chop or mince the meat finely. Chop the onion finely. Put the meat and onion into a pan with the ketchup, parsley, salt and pepper, and just cover with water or stock. Simmer gently until the meat is tender. Mix 1 tablespoon flour with a little cold water and stir into the pan. Simmer for 5 minutes, and then leave until cold.

Sieve the flour and salt into a bowl. Put the lard, milk and water into a pan and bring to the boil. Tip in the flour and mix well to form soft pastry. Knead until smooth, and cool slightly. Cut off one-third of the pastry and keep on one side. Roll out the remaining pastry and cut out four 7 in (17.5cm) circles. Place on a greased baking-sheet and mould each circle up round a jam jar to give a 2 in (5cm) wall.

Preheat oven to 190°C/375°F/Gas Mark 5. Fill each pastry case with meat. Roll out remaining pastry and cut out lids. Place lids on the pies and pinch edges together firmly. Cut a small hole in the centre of each lid. Bake for 40 minutes. Heat any left-over gravy and pour through the holes in the pie lids. Eat very hot.

Aberdeen Sausage

Serves 4–6

1 lb (450g) stewing steak
4 oz (100g) streaky bacon
4 oz (100g) onions
4 oz (100g) porridge oats
a little brown sauce
1 egg
1 teaspoon salt
ground black pepper
1 tablespoon chopped fresh parsley

Preheat oven to 150°C/300°F/Gas Mark 2.
Put the beef, bacon and onions twice
through the mincer, or chop finely in a
food processor. Add the
remaining ingredients
and mix well. Shape
into a fat sausage and
wrap in foil that has been
lightly brushed with
oil. Place on a
baking-sheet
and bake for
2 hours. Cool
in foil for
10 minutes.
Unwrap on to
a serving-dish.
If liked, the
cooked sausage may
be lightly coated with
fine brown breadcrumbs.

This economical
meat loaf, made from
good Scottish beef,
bacon and oats, is
quite solid and easy
to slice, and is good
with salad or pickles.
The sausage may be
eaten hot with gravy
and vegetables.

Venison Casserole

VENISON CASSEROLE

SERVES 4

2 lb (1 kg) venison
2 oz (50g) lard or dripping
2 oz (50 g) bacon
3 medium carrots
2 medium onions
1 oz (25g) plain flour
1/2 pint (300ml) beef stock
1/2 pint (300ml) red wine
sprig of thyme
sprig of parsley
sprig of rosemary
1 bay leaf
1 garlic clove
pinch of ground allspice
salt and freshly ground black pepper
2 tablespoons redcurrant jelly

Venison makes a richly flavoured casserole with plenty of herbs and spices. Red deer is tougher and needs longer to cook, but roe deer is tender. Farmed deer is also more tender than the wild variety.

Cube the meat and brown lightly in hot lard or dripping. Remove to a casserole. Dice the bacon and slice the carrots and onions. Cook in the fat until golden, and transfer to the casserole. Work the flour into the pan juices and cook for 1 minute. Add the stock and wine and stir over low heat until smooth. Pour over the meat and vegetables. Add the herbs, crushed garlic, allspice and plenty of salt and pepper.

Cover and cook gently for about 2½ hours until tender. Stir in the redcurrant jelly and continue cooking for 10 minutes. Serve with boiled potatoes and green or root vegetables.

The name derives from the early use of 'to stove' as a verb indicating that a dish was cooked on or in the stove very gently. The dish usually consisted of a complete one-pot meal so that no further preparation was needed during cooking. The English equivalent is a hotpot.

STOVED CHICKEN
SERVES 4

4 chicken joints
2 tablespoons plain flour
salt and pepper
2 oz (50g) butter
2 lb (1kg) potatoes
1 lb (450g) onions
1/2 pint (300ml) water or chicken stock
chopped fresh parsley

Preheat oven to 180°C/350°F/Gas Mark 4. Coat the chicken joints with flour that has been well-seasoned with salt and pepper. Brown lightly in the butter. Peel and slice the potatoes and onions.

Put a layer of potatoes and onions in an ovenware dish and put two chicken joints on top. Add another layer of potatoes and onions, seasoning well with salt and pepper. Put on remaining chicken and cover with a final layer of potatoes. Season well and pour over the buttery juices from the frying-pan. Pour in water or stock. Cover and cook for 1 1/2 hours. Take off the lid and continue cooking until potatoes are golden-brown. Sprinkle with parsley.

Stoved Chicken

Young well-hung grouse are essential for roasting, and they should be served in the classic manner with game chips, fried breadcrumbs and bread sauce. Grouse is particularly good paired with the slightly sharp flavour of cranberries or rowan-berries, so the appropriate sauce or jelly may be served. Some cooks like to put a few berries inside the birds before roasting.

ROAST GROUSE
SERVES 4

4 young grouse
1 oz (25g) butter
2 teaspoons lemon juice
salt and freshly ground black pepper
8 rashers streaky bacon
2 slices bread
grouse livers
butter for spreading
pinch of Cayenne pepper

Preheat oven to 190°C/375°F/Gas Mark 5. Put grouse in a roasting-tin. Mix the butter with lemon juice and plenty of salt and pepper. Place a little inside each bird. Cover each bird with 2 bacon rashers. Roast for 30 minutes, removing the bacon for the last 5 minutes so that the breasts brown. Grouse must not be overcooked.

Toast the bread slices on one side only and cut each in half. Simmer the livers in a little water for 10 minutes. Drain well and mash with a little butter, seasoning with salt and Cayenne pepper. Spread on the untoasted side of bread slices, and serve a bird on each slice.

STUFFED AYRSHIRE ROLL
SERVES 6

3 lb (1.5kg) rolled joint streaky bacon
2 oz (50g) butter
4 oz (100g) fresh white breadcrumbs
2 tablespoons chopped fresh parsley
2 teaspoons chopped fresh thyme
grated rind of 1 lemon
1 egg
freshly ground black pepper

Put the bacon joint into a pan and just cover with cold water. Bring to the boil and then cover and simmer for 40 minutes. Drain well and remove string. Unroll the bacon, and strip off and discard the rind.

Preheat oven to 180°C/350°F/Gas Mark 4. Melt the butter and stir in the breadcrumbs, herbs, lemon rind and egg, and season well with pepper. Put in the centre of the bacon and roll up again firmly, tying with string. Score the fat in a criss-cross pattern. Put into a roasting-tin and cook for 1 hour. Serve hot with potatoes and vegetables, or cold with pickles.

A rolled joint of streaky bacon is transformed by a herb stuffing and becomes succulent when roasted. The herbs may be varied. Marjoram, sage and rosemary are all additions for a special occasion. Include a few soaked prunes or some chopped apples in the stuffing.

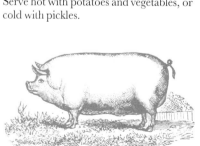

VEGETABLE DISHES

The Scots have not been able to produce large quantities of salad vegetables because of their soil and climate, but they have always been successful at growing root vegetables and potatoes. The latter are grown in a huge variety, and great attention is paid as to whether a waxy or floury potato is needed for a recipe.

This is an Orkney vegetable dish that is delicious on its own with some extra butter, but excellent also with meat, fish or poultry, and particularly haggis.

CLAPSHOT
SERVES 4

1 lb (450g) potatoes
1 lb (450g) turnips
1 oz (25g) chives
1 oz (25g) butter
salt and pepper

Peel and boil the potatoes and the turnips. Drain well and mash together. Add chopped chives, butter and plenty of seasoning. Serve very hot.

RUMBLEDETHUMPS
SERVES 4

1 lb (450g) potatoes
1 lb (450g) cabbage
2 oz (50g) butter
1 medium onion
1 tablespoon chopped chives
2 oz (50g) grated cheese

Boil the potatoes, drain well and mash.
Cook the cabbage, drain well and mix
with the potatoes. Melt the butter and
add finely chopped onion. Cook for about
5 minutes until softened but not browned.
Add to the potatoes and cabbage with the
cooking-juices and mix with the chives.
Season well and pile into a pie-dish.
Sprinkle with grated cheese and brown
under a hot grill. Serve at once, sprinkled
with some extra chopped chives.

A splendid vegetable
dish to eat with meat
or poultry, but it is
delicious on its own.
To 'thump' is to
'bash', and 'rumbled'
is 'mixed', which
gives the unusual and
delightful name to
a simple dish.
The type of cabbage
may be varied for
a different texture
and flavour. Savoy
cabbage, kale or
Brussels sprouts are
all very tasty in
this mixture.

Crannachan

PUDDINGS

There are not many puddings in the Scottish cook's recipe books, perhaps because they had so many baked goods on breakfast and tea tables. Main puddings are either boiled or baked suet puddings, relieved by dried fruit, or delicious but simple mixtures of cream or cream cheese with raspberries and often a dusting of crunchy oats.

CRANNACHAN

SERVES 4

2 oz (50g) medium oatmeal
5 tablespoons whisky
2 tablespoons thick honey
2 oz (50g) cream cheese
4 oz (100g) raspberries
1/4 pint (150ml) double cream
4 teaspoons clear honey

Put the oatmeal, whisky and thick honey in a bowl and leave to stand overnight. Mix in the cream cheese and fold in the raspberries. Whisk the cream to soft peaks and put half of it in the bases of 4 wine glasses. Spoon in the whisky mixture and top with the remaining cream. Make a small well in the centre of each topping and pour in the clear honey. Chill for 30 minutes before serving.

This used to be made for Hallowe'en and Harvest, with charms mixed into it, which would be eagerly sought by children. There are simpler recipes, but this version is rich and delicious. Start preparing on the day before you want to eat it.

This dish is also known as Cream Crowdie. 'Crowdie' was a porridge of oatmeal and water, and the addition of cream and local low-fat cheese made it very special.

Wild blackberries, known as 'brambles', are popular in Scotland and lend their distinctive flavour to puddings, jams and jellies.

DUNFILLAN PUDDING

SERVES 4

1 lb (450g) blackberries
6 tablespoons water
4 oz (100g) sugar

Topping
2 oz (50g) butter
2 oz (50g) caster sugar
1 egg
4 oz (100g) self-raising flour
pinch of salt
2 tablespoons milk
1 teaspoon grated lemon rind
caster sugar for sprinkling

Preheat oven to 180°C/350°F/Gas Mark 4. Wash the blackberries and put into a pan with the water. Simmer until soft and sweeten with the sugar. Put into a pie-dish. Cream the butter and caster sugar together and work in the egg. Sieve the flour and salt together and fold into the creamed mixture. Fold in the milk and lemon rind. Spread over the blackberries and bake for 30 minutes. Sprinkle with caster sugar and serve hot with cream or custard.

CLOUTIE DUMPLING

SERVES 8

1 lb (450g) plain flour
6 oz (150g) fresh breadcrumbs
8 oz (225g) sultanas
8 oz (225g) currants
4 oz (100g) raisins
4 oz (100g) chopped mixed peel
8 oz (225g) dark soft brown sugar
8 oz (225g) black treacle
8 oz (225g) shredded suet
2 teaspoons ground cinnamon
2 teaspoons ground ginger
2 teaspoons ground mixed spice
1 teaspoon baking-powder
½ teaspoon salt
2 eating-apples, grated
2 medium carrots, grated
2 eggs
grated zest and juice of 1 lemon
a little milk

Mix all the ingredients well, and if necessary add a little milk to make a soft consistency.

Half-fill a large pan with water and bring to the boil. Put in a large piece of clean white cloth. Lift out and drain well, then spread the cloth on a flat surface. Flour lightly to form a seal. Put on pudding mixture and draw up edges. Tie with string and leave a little room for expansion. Put a plate upside down in the pan and place the dumpling on top. Bring to a simmer, cover and simmer for 3 hours.

Unroll on to a plate and dry in low oven for 10 minutes. Sprinkle with caster sugar before serving hot, with cream or custard if liked.

Named from the cloth in which it is cooked, this is rather like a cannon-ball Christmas pudding. It is particularly popular at Hogmanay (New Year's Eve), being tasty and filling. Left-over pudding is cut into slices which may be eaten like cake or fried with the breakfast bacon. There is a knack to preparing the pudding cloth in which it is cooked, but the mixture may be prepared in a bowl although it will not look traditional. There are many recipes for this delicacy, and this one is similar to a rich but light Christmas pudding.

Tillypronie Honey Cakes (page 36)
and Treacle Scones

BREADS, CAKES AND BISCUITS

The Scots have always had a sweet tooth, perhaps because so much sugar was imported, and partly perhaps to offset the early plain diet of oats, herrings and potatoes. The Scots are great bakers, using the early bakestone or griddle, and later the oven, to produce a delectable range of breads, savoury and sweet biscuits, and cakes. Breakfast is always very good in a Scottish household with its array of 'bakes', but teatime is a sight to behold.

TREACLE SCONES

8 oz (225g) self-raising flour
pinch of salt
$^1/_2$ teaspoon bicarbonate of soda
1 teaspoon ground mixed spice
$^1/_2$ oz (15g) dark soft brown sugar
1 oz (25g) butter
2 tablespoons black treacle
$^3/_4$ pint (150ml) milk

These dark spiced scones are a favourite variation on the traditional Scottish scone.

Flour a baking-sheet lightly. Preheat oven to 220°C/425°F/Gas Mark 7. Sift together the flour, salt, soda and spice, and stir in the sugar. Rub in the butter until the mixture is like coarse breadcrumbs. Mix with the treacle and milk to give a soft dough. Roll out on a floured board to $^1/_2$ in (1.25cm) thick. Cut into 2 in (5cm) rounds with a plain cutter. Put the scones on to the baking-sheet so that they just touch each other. Bake for 15 minutes. Cool on a wire rack, and serve split and buttered.

35

Heather honey is delicious and is frequently used in recipes. These biscuits, from a 19th-century recipe, are particularly delectable.

TILLYPRONIE HONEY CAKES

1 lb (450g) plain flour
1¹/₂ teaspoons baking-powder
pinch of salt
4 oz (100g) butter
2 tablespoons heather honey
2 tablespoons caster sugar
2 egg yolks
¹/₂ pint (300ml) milk

Topping
1 egg white
4 oz (100g) thick heather honey
3 tablespoons ground almonds

Preheat oven to 180°C/350°F/Gas Mark 4. Grease two baking-sheets. Sieve the flour, baking-powder and salt into a bowl. Rub in the butter until the mixture is like fine breadcrumbs. Mix together the honey, sugar, egg yolks and milk and work into the dry ingredients. Mix to a firm dough and roll out lightly on a floured board.

Cut into 2 in (5cm) rounds and place on baking-sheets. Bake for 20 minutes. Lower oven heat to 150°C/300°F/Gas Mark 2. Brush tops of biscuits with egg white. Mix honey and ground almonds and spread on biscuits. Continue baking for 4 minutes. Serve hot or cold. Makes 24 biscuits.

SHORTBREAD

4 oz (100g) plain flour
2 oz (50g) rice flour or cornflour
4 oz (100g) butter
2 oz (50g) caster sugar

Preheat oven to 180°C/350°F/Gas Mark 4.
Sieve the flour and rice flour or cornflour on
to a board. Cut the butter into pieces and
mix with the sugar in a
separate pile. Work
the butter and
sugar together
with the hands
and gradually
work in the flour
to make a firm
dough. Form
into a ball and
roll out on a
lightly floured
surface to a
circle 8 in
(20cm) in
diameter.
Lift on to a
greased baking-
sheet and pinch the
edges between finger and thumb. Prick
lightly all over with a fork. Bake for
10 minutes. Lower oven heat to 160°C/
325°F/Gas Mark 3 and continue baking for
25 minutes. Leave on the baking-sheet and
mark into triangular wedges. After 5 minutes,
lift on to a wire rack to cool. Sprinkle with a
little caster sugar before serving.

Meltingly delicious
butter shortbread is
one of the most
popular specialities
from Scotland.
Sometimes it is
shaped in a wooden
mould with a thistle
design. The addition
of rice flour or
cornflour gives a
crisp short texture.

37

LEMON SCOTCH CAKE

A light cake with a distinctive flavour of lemon and whisky that epitomises the best of Scots baking.

4 oz (100g) butter
4 oz (100g) caster sugar
2 tablespoons lemon curd
2 eggs
6 oz (150g) seedless raisins
6 tablespoons whisky
6 oz (150g) self-raising flour

Preheat oven to 180°C/350°F/Gas Mark 4. Grease and base-line a 7 in (17.5cm) square cake tin. Cream the butter, sugar and lemon curd until light and fluffy. Separate the eggs and beat the yolks into the creamed mixture, adding a little flour so that the mixture does not curdle.

Add raisins and whisky with a little more flour and then fold in remaining flour. Whisk the egg whites to soft peaks and fold into the mixture. Put into the prepared tin and bake for 1 1/4 hours. Cool in the tin for 5 minutes, and turn on to a wire rack to cool.

Dundee Cake (page 40)
and Lemon Scotch Cake

A light orange flavour is characteristic of this cake, so maybe it was a by-product of the marmalade industry which originated in Dundee.

DUNDEE CAKE

8 oz (225g) butter
8 oz (225g) caster sugar
5 eggs
8 oz (225g) self-raising flour
$1/2$ teaspoon grated nutmeg
3 oz (75g) glacé cherries
grated rind of 1 orange
grated rind of 1 lemon
6 oz (150g) currants
6 oz (150g) sultanas
2 oz (50g) chopped mixed candied peel
3 oz (75g) ground almonds
3 oz (75g) blanched almonds

Grease a 10 in (25cm) round cake tin. Preheat the oven to 160°C/325°F/Gas Mark 3. Cream the butter and sugar together until light and fluffy. Add the eggs one at a time with a teaspoon of flour and beat well after each addition. Sift the remaining flour with the nutmeg and fold into the creamed mixture.

Rinse and dry the cherries and cut them into quarters. Fold in the orange and lemon rinds, currants, sultanas, cherries and peel and mix well. Finally, fold in the ground almonds. Put the cake mixture into the tin and slightly hollow the centre with the back of a spoon. Bake for 1$1/2$ hours. Gently draw the cake part-way out of the oven and quickly and lightly arrange the almonds on top in circles. Return the cake to the oven and continue baking for 1 hour. Leave to cool in the tin for 10 minutes and then turn on to a wire rack to finish cooling.

Fochabers Gingerbread

8 oz (225g) butter
4 oz (100g) light soft brown sugar
8 oz (225g) black treacle
2 eggs
1 lb (450g) plain flour
1 oz (25g) ground mixed spice
1/2 oz (15g) ground ginger
pinch of ground cloves
pinch of ground cinnamon
4 oz (100g) currants
4 oz (100g) sultanas
3 oz (75g) chopped mixed candied peel
3 oz (75g) ground almonds
1 teaspoon bicarbonate of soda
1/2 pint (300ml) beer

Grease and line a 9 in (22.5 cm) round
cake tin. Preheat oven to 160°C/325°F/
Gas Mark 3. Cream the butter and sugar
until light and fluffy. Warm the treacle
until just runny and beat into the fat
mixture. Beat in the eggs. Sieve the flour
and spices and stir into the mixture with
the dried fruit and almonds. Dissolve the
soda in the beer and beat into the
mixture. Put into the tin and bake for
2 hours. Leave in the tin for 15 minutes,
and turn on to a wire rack to cool.

This is gingerbread
for a special occasion,
since it is richer than
many recipes and
also contains dried
fruit. The additional
spices enhance the
flavour of ginger.

SWEET THINGS

Delicious baked goods need delectable spreads, and every housewife has her cupboard full of honey, marmalade and a selection of soft-fruit jams that are served at breakfast and at teatime. She also likes to spoil her family with home-made sweetmeats like toffee, butterscotch and tablet, and with honey-based drinks.

The distinctive rowan tree, with its clusters of bright orange berries, grows well in Scotland, and jelly made from the fruit is particularly popular eaten with game. The berries should be used before they change from orange to dark red, at which time they become bitter.

ROWAN JELLY

2 lb (1kg) just ripe rowan-berries
2 lb (1kg) cooking-apples
sugar

Discard any stems from the berries, and put the fruit into a large pan. Do not peel the apples, but chop them roughly and add to the berries. Just cover with water and simmer until tender. Strain through a jelly bag, leaving until the juice has stopped dripping. Do not squeeze the bag or the juice will be cloudy. Measure the juice, and allow 1 pint (600ml) to each lb (450g) sugar. Simmer together over low heat so that the sugar dissolves. Boil rapidly, stirring occasionally, and removing any scum when necessary. After 10 minutes of hard boiling, test for setting. Drop a spoonful on a cold plate and leave until cool. Push gently with the finger and the surface of the jelly will wrinkle when the setting-point has been reached. Pour into small clean dry jars that have been heated. Cover and label.

ATHOLL BROSE

6 oz (150g) medium oatmeal
¹/₁ pint (150ml) water
2 tablespoons heather honey
1¹/₂ pints (750ml) whisky

Put the oatmeal and water into a small bowl
and mix to form a paste. Leave for 1 hour
and then put through a fine sieve to press out
all the liquid. Stir the honey into the liquid
and put into a large bottle. Fill up with
whisky and seal well. Shake well to mix.
Always shake well before drinking.

A very satisfying
alcoholic drink that
combines three
essential ingredients
in the Scottish diet:
oatmeal, whisky and
honey. It is a
celebration drink
enjoyed particularly
at Hogmanay.

TABLET

3 pints (1.8 litres) water
8 oz (225g) butter
4 lb (2kg) sugar
1 lb (450g) sweetened condensed milk

Put the water and butter into a deep thick
pan and heat gently until the butter has
melted. Stir in the sugar and bring to the boil,
stirring slowly all the time. When the mixture
is boiling, add the condensed milk. Simmer
for 25 minutes, only stirring occasionally to
prevent sticking. Take off heat and stir in
chosen flavouring. Beat hard for 5 minutes
and pour into a greased tin. Leave for
5 minutes and mark into squares or bars.
Cut and remove when cold.

The Scots have a
passion for 'sweeties',
perhaps because their
traditional diet was
rather bland and
heavy, but also
because huge
quantities of sugar
came into the great
ports. Tablet is a
special favourite,
being a rich fudge-
toffee flavoured with
spices, peppermint,
vanilla, lemon
or orange.

Marmalade

Marmalade

2 lb (1kg) Seville oranges
4 pints (2 litres) water
1 lemon
4 lb (2kg) sugar

Wipe the fruit and cut oranges in half.
Squeeze out juice and pips. Tie pips into
a piece of muslin to suspend in a large
preserving-pan. Put orange juice in the pan
with the water and juice of the lemon. Slice
the peel thinly and add to the pan.

Simmer for about 1 1/2 hours until the peel
is soft and the liquid is reduced by half. Take
out the bag of pips and squeeze out any
liquid into the pan. Stir in the sugar over low
heat until dissolved. Boil rapidly to setting-
point. To test for setting, pour a spoonful
on to a cold saucer, then leave to cool for
2–3 minutes. If the mixture wrinkles when
pushed with a finger, it is ready for setting.
Cool for 15 minutes.
Stir well, put
into hot jars
and cover.

Marmalade is a
Scottish invention, as
the first jars were
made on a
commercial basis by
Mrs Keiller of
Dundee, whose
merchant husband
had to make use of an
unwanted cargo of
bitter oranges. The
name is said to derive
from *marmelo*, which
is the Portuguese
word for 'quince', a
fruit that was widely
grown and imported
and made into a thick
preserve with wine,
honey and spices
well-boiled to make
an almost leathery
paste that stored well.